It's Fun to Draw
Knights and Castles

Mark Bergin

WINDMILL
BOOKS

New York

Published in 2012 by Windmill Books, LLC
303 Park Avenue South, Suite #1280, New York, NY 10010-3657

Editor: Rob Walker
U.S. Editor: Sara Antill

Library of Congress Cataloging-in-Publication Data

Bergin, Mark.
 Knights and castles / by Mark Bergin. — 1st ed.
    p. cm. — (It's fun to draw)
 Includes index.
 ISBN 978-1-61533-352-3 (library binding)
 1. Knights and knighthood in art—Juvenile literature. 2. Castles in art—Juvenile literature. 3. Drawing—Technique—Juvenile literature. I. Title.

NC825.K54B473 2012
741.2—dc22

2010052109

Manufactured in Heshan, China

CPSIA Compliance Information: Batch #SS1102WM:
For Further Information contact Windmill Books, New York,
New York at 1-866-478-0556

Contents

Castle Guard

1 Start with the helmet. Add eye slots and dots for breathing holes.

2 Add a shield. Draw markings on it.

You Can Do It!

Use a black felt-tip pen for the lines. Add color using watercolor paint.

3 Draw a rectangle for the body and add legs.

4 Add the arm holding a spear.

5 Draw a belt and a scabbard.

Splat-a-Fact!

Important knights lived in castles.

Eagleford Castle

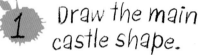

1 Draw the main castle shape.

2 Draw two lines and add the gateway.

You Can Do It!

Use a blue felt-tip pen for the lines. Add color using pencils.

3 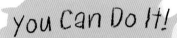 Draw the ramparts.

4 Add a drawbridge and iron gate.

5 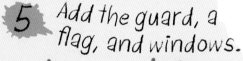 Add the guard, a flag, and windows.

Splat-a-Fact!
The moat and drawbridge kept the castle safe from enemies.

7

Norman Knight

 1 Start with the shield.

2 Add the tunic.

 **3** Draw the head with a mouth and a dot for the eye. Add a pointed helmet.

Splat-a-Fact!
Norman knights won the Battle of Hastings in the year 1066.

You Can Do It!
Use wax crayons for the color and a black felt-tip pen for the lines.

4 Draw an arm holding a sword.

 5 Add the legs.

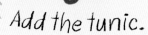

9

Ax Knight

1 Cut out a helmet. Draw a slit and breathing holes. Glue it on colored paper.

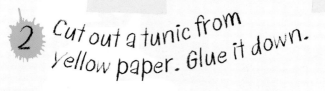

2 Cut out a tunic from yellow paper. Glue it down.

3 Tear out the shield shape and glue it down. Tear out a red cross and add it to the shield.

Splat-a-Fact!

Knights could fight with an ax or just throw it at the enemy.

You Can Do It!

Cut out the knight's armor shapes from tin foil. Use a marker pen for the details.

4 Cut out legs. Glue them down. Add detail.

5 Cut out an arm and the ax head. Cut out the handle. Glue them down. Add details.

Make sure you get an adult to help you when using scissors!

Archer

1 Start with the head. Add a helmet, mouth, and a dot for the eye.

2 Add the body and arms.

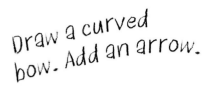

3 Draw a curved bow. Add an arrow.

4 Add a quiver and a belt.

5 Draw the legs and feet. Finish details.

You Can Do It!

Use crayons for all textures. Then paint over the picture with watercolors. Try using a sponge to dab on the paint.

Splat-a-Fact!
Archers stood on top
of castle walls and
shot at the enemy.

13

Ravenswood Castle

Start with a square and add a gateway.

2 Draw the towers and add windows.

You Can Do It!
Use a soft pencil for the lines and add color using watercolor paint.

Splat-a-Fact!
A castle's main gate was very strong. It was often a thick, iron-studded, wooden door.

3 Draw in triangles for the pointed roofs.

4 Add finishing details, such as windows, doors, and battlements.

15

Jousting Tent

1 Start with the top of the tent. Add a wavy line.

2 Draw the tent with a gap for the entrance.

3 Add stripes and a flag.

Splat-a-Fact!
The knight's jousting tent was where he got ready for the tournament.

4 Draw the knight's colors on the flag and banner.

16

Jousting Knight

1

Start with the horse's head and body.

You Can Do It!

Use a pencil for the lines. Use a white crayon to make textures. Then paint over the drawing with watercolor paint.

2 Add the eyes, nostrils, and hooves.

3

Draw the knight with a helmet. Add his legs on either side of the horse.

4 Add a lance and shield. Draw feathers on the helmet.

Splat-a-Fact!

It took about 14 years to train to be a knight.

18

19

The Joust

1 Start with the horse's head and coat.

2 Add its eyes, mouth, tail, and hooves.

You Can Do It!
Use a brown felt-tip pen for the lines. Add color with colored felt-tip pens.

3 Draw the knight with a shield.

4 Draw the reins and a saddle. Add detail to the coat.

5 Add a lance and a feather on the helmet.

Splat-a-Fact!
A knight needed a lot of money. A shiny suit of armor was very expensive!

21

Mace Knight

1 Start with the helmet shape. Add a visor with dots for breathing holes and two slits for the eyes.

2 Add the knight's tunic and shield.

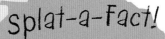

Splat-a-Fact!

A knight wore his colors on his tunic and shield to show who was inside the suit of armor.

3 Add a belt and the legs.

4 Draw the arm holding a mace.

You Can Do It!

Use colored pencils and a black felt-tip pen for the lines. Smudge or blend the color for more interest.

Hawkbury Castle

1 Cut out the middle section of the castle. Glue it down.

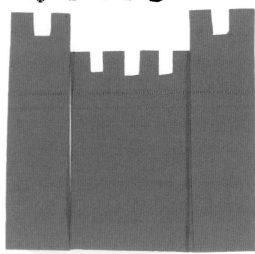

2 Cut out two towers. Glue them down.

you Can Do It!

Cut out the shapes from colored paper. Glue them onto a sheet of blue paper. Use a felt-tip pen for the lines.

3 Draw windows and a doorway.

4 Add a guard and a large banner on top.

24

Make sure you get an adult to help you when using scissors!

splat-a-fact!
The walls of a castle are very high to stop attackers from climbing in.

25

Arabian Knight

1 Start with the tunic and a round shield. Add details.

2 Add the head, with dots for the eyes, a nose, and a mustache.

3 Add the helmet shape.

You Can Do It!

Use a white crayon to create textures. Then paint over your picture with watercolor paint. Use a pencil for the lines.

4 Draw an arm holding a curved sword.

5 Add the scabbard. Draw the legs.

spearman

1

Start with the helmet and the head. Add dots for the eyes and a mouth.

2

Add the tunic.

3

Draw the arm and spear.

you Can Do It!

Use a brown felt-tip pen for the lines and add color with soft, chalky pastels. Smudge and blend some of the colors to add interest.

Splat-a-Fact!

In battle, the spearman could keep enemies at a safe distance with his long spear.

4 Add a long shield shape.

5 Draw the legs.

29

Battling Knight

1
Start with the helmet. Add slits for the eyes and a pointed beak shape.

you Can do it!
Use crayons for texture. Then paint over your drawing with watercolor paint. Use a felt-tip pen for the lines.

2 Add a shield with a cross.

3 Draw a belted tunic with a cross on it.

4
Draw the legs and the armor.

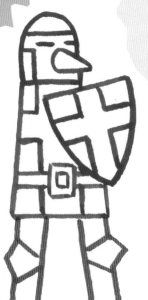

5 Add an arm holding a sword.